Perthshire

Perthshire

By

Allan Wright

First Published in Great Britain by

Lyrical Scotland, an Imprint of Cauldron Press Ltd
Parton House Stables
Castle Douglas
Kirkcudbrightshire
Scotland
DG7 3NB

www.lyricalscotland.com

ISBN13: 978-1-905683-18-5

British Library Cataloguing-in-Publication Data

A catalogue record for this book is available on request from the British Library

Jacket design by Isobel Bathgate
Layout and captions by Allan Wright
Page make up by Small Print, Castle Douglas
Printed by Ozgraf, Poland

Preface

Perthshire has for me always presented the most captivating and diverse of landscapes; Rolling rugged, colourful and serene it is possesses an intense mix of all that is best about Scotland. It is big loch, big tree and big river country and in 15 years of tramping around it has always impressed me and you can be sure that any investment of time and energy spent here will be thoroughly rewarded.

I detect it has a special sense of itself, in contrast to say the West Coast with its tumbledown and more laissez-faire style, Perthshire does a more manicured thing. At worst it could be accused of taking itself a little seriously but then wouldn't you if you had its looks. Very little of "Scotland's County" qualifies as untouched but then neither has it been much spoiled. The tree is the element which fuses this landscape together, Perthshire's trees are stunning, bountiful and have clearly been revered by generations of guardians who have dwelled and evolved this landscape in partnership with them. If the trees and mountains don't get you then the elegant country houses and or the pastoral qualities of the glens, gardens and meadows will. This seductively beautiful area of Scotland, like the school heart-throb, is likely to get a grip on you, so be warned.

This photo essay is the culmination of countless short visits to the County and in essence it has to be a personal vision and inevitably I concede there are bound to be omissions. Nonetheless I have tried to include all the principal landmarks and features plus some more subtle details. There is no obvious way to tackle Perthshire, you could jump into it just about anywhere and this is reflected in the fact there is no strict sequence to these images i.e. the journey starts in the South, goes East, then North and meanders up and down the Lochs to the West, to end up back in the South. Enjoy.

Allan Wright

July 2007

Introduction

Perthshire not only lies at the heart of Scotland, it also encompasses all that is best about the country. Its varied scenery ranges from the awe-inspiring to the intimate, and contains hills, moors, trees, animals and buildings that are characteristically Scottish.

However, it would be wrong to think of this as 'Scotland in miniature' because nothing here is on a small scale. Quite the reverse; Perthshire is known as the 'big county' – it covers a large area and is famed for its tall trees, impressive mountains, long lochs and mighty rivers.

In this book, Allan has captured Perthshire's magnificent and diverse scenery. Through his photographs, you can enjoy the beauty of Glen Lyon, wonder at the height of the Meikleour Beech Hedge and experience the splendour of Scone Palace. The pictures take you into the heart of the landscape to enjoy many beautiful places.

These images, like the administrative area of Perth and Kinross, encompass a wide area. The scope ranges from Loch Earn in the west to the outskirts of Dundee in the east, and from Kinross, on the shores of Loch Leven, to the Drumochter Pass, 70 miles further north. I hope that, in bringing aspects of Perthshire alive, they will inspire you to visit or revisit the places so vividly portrayed.

As you browse the photographs, you'll enjoy every type of Scottish scenery, except dramatic seascapes. The rugged mountains, high heather moorland and steep-sided glens of Highland Perthshire have a grandeur that will make your heart soar. Or you can experience an unrivalled sense of open space by gazing at Rannoch Moor's miles of wilderness.

By contrast, southern Perthshire and Kinross-shire have a lowland landscape, with wide, fertile valleys and rolling green hills. There is still a feeling of spaciousness, but it is a gentler environment where humankind has made more of a mark. Country lanes wind through tree-lined fields, linking villages of terraced sandstone houses. The mature policy woodlands and formal gardens surrounding the many castles and big houses contribute to the splendid views.

Perthshire may lack sea cliffs and sandy beaches, but it is not landlocked. Its major river, the Tay, flows into a wide estuary, or Firth, which has reed beds of national importance. The river is tidal to above Perth – the city has its own harbour and grey seals are sometimes seen from the riverside boulevard of Tay Street, some 30 miles from the open sea.

With its many substantial tributaries, the River Tay drains 3,000 square miles of the southern Highlands – a larger area than any other Scottish river – and it discharges more water into the sea than any river in Britain. Its watershed matches, by and large, the boundary of Perthshire and runs along the crest of some of the county's highest mountains, which rise to over 1000m. The Tay and its tributaries, including the Earn, Almond, Braan, Tummel, Garry, Isla and Ericht, are top class salmon and trout fishing rivers. Their clear, fast flowing waters provide an ideal habitat for a wide range of wildlife, from dipper, duck and osprey to the elusive otter.

These pure waters provide the most important raw material for the county's five whisky distilleries. In Perthshire, you will find the smallest distillery in Scotland – Edradour near Pitlochry – and the oldest – Glenturret in Crieff, which was built in 1775 and is now home to the Famous Grouse Experience. Moreover, one of the world's most famous brands of bottled water – Highland Spring – is sourced from springs in the Ochil Hills.

Another use for Perthshire's lochs and rivers has been the generation of power. In the 1950s very extensive hydroelectric schemes were built in the catchments of the Garry and Tummel, north of Pitlochry, and the Turret and Lednock rivers, west of Crieff. The power stations were blended into the landscape – sometimes being put underground – and today few people notice much of the infrastructure, apart from Pitlochry Dam, which is a tourist attraction in its own right, and pretty Loch Faskally, which is a man-made reservoir.

During the last Ice Age, which ended some 10,000 years ago, the whole of this area was covered in thick ice. In Highland Perthshire, the glaciers gouged deep U-shaped glens out of the hard, metamorphic rocks. Rivers now follow the course of these glens, with lochs filling the deepest trenches. When you look at the long, sinuous shapes of Lochs Rannoch, Tummel, Tay and Earn, remember the great glaciers that once filled these valleys.

In Kinross-shire and lowland Perthshire, the harder volcanic rocks of the Ochil, Sidlaw, Lomond and Cleish hill ranges provided some resistance to the ice, but the softer sandstone rocks in between were ground down, leaving wide valleys or 'straths'. When the ice retreated, it left sedimentary deposits on these plains, which today are fertile farmland. One interesting phenomena was caused by a large mass of ice that remained in the south long after the main ice sheet had melted. This left a depression that is now filled by the almost circular Loch Leven – a gleaming jewel in the green landscape.

After the Ice Age, Perthshire was re-colonised by plants and animals. What we now consider our native trees, such as birch, rowan, Scots pine, alder, ash and oak, spread along the river valleys and up the hillsides. A wide range of birds and mammals found their home here, from the iconic golden eagle and magnificent red deer, to the small but colourful Scottish crossbill and seldom-seen wildcat.

The human species soon followed, attracted by the abundance of fish, game and wild food plants. Arriving over 8,000 years ago, the Mesolithic hunter-gatherers were the first to exploit the area. They left few traces beyond their flint tools. The earliest monuments you can see around the landscape of Perthshire date from 6,000 years ago and are the long cairns, cup-marked rocks and standing stones of the more settled Neolithic farmers. The stone circle at Croft Moraig, near Kenmore, is a prime example. In turn, the peoples of the Bronze and Iron Ages left their mark, with roundhouses and field systems on the lower ground, and the numerous forts that are still visible on the prominent summits of the hills.

The attractiveness and diversity of this area has made it a focal point since prehistoric times. For, as well as being geographically at the heart of the Scotland, Perthshire is also central to its history – both as the birthplace of the country and as the site of momentous events. Tour around the county and the places you visit will provide a condensed history of Scotland, seasoned by the drama of heroic triumphs and defeats.

The earliest written history dates from the Roman invasion of Scotland in the first century AD. Although Hadrian's Wall and the Antonine Wall are more famous, the first and most northerly frontier of the Roman Empire was the Gask Ridge, which runs through south Perthshire. A road was built here and marked at approximately every kilometre by a signal station, while elsewhere around Perthshire there are the remains of several large forts, big enough for thousands of soldiers.

It appears that the Pictish tribes the Romans encountered in Perthshire proved too difficult to control, and, after several decades, the legions retreated further south. Over the next few hundred years this Pictish society gradually developed, but we know little about them and their beliefs beyond the enigmatic symbols and patterns they left in beautifully carved stones, like the one at Fowlis Wester. During the Pictish era, the first Christian missionaries came to Perthshire and began to convert the people. Among them was St Serf, who left his name on an island in Loch Leven and a church in Dunning, Strathearn.

In 844 AD, the unified Scottish kingdom was founded when Kenneth MacAlpin brought together the rival kingdoms of the Scots, who ruled Dalraida in the west, and the Picts, who held sway in the east and north. He established his capital at Forteviot in Strathearn, making Perthshire the power-base of the Scottish monarchs. For many centuries Scotland's kings and queens were crowned at Scone, seated on the Stone of Destiny, which was brought from Iona.

The early years of the Scottish nation were turbulent and bloody; more kings died by the sword than met a natural death. Among them was Macbeth, whose connection with Perthshire was immortalised by Shakespeare. His downfall came when he was overpowered in his hill-fort at Dunsinane in the Sidlaw Hills after seeing what appeared to be Birnam Wood moving across the valley. Too late, he realised it was advancing soldiers using branches cut from the trees for disguise.

One of the greatest challenges of the time was to maintain Scotland's independence from its larger neighbour, England. Much of the struggle took place on Perthshire soil. Symbolically, the biggest blow came when Edward I invaded and stole the Stone of Destiny from Scone, taking it south to Westminster Abbey.

Resistance to the English overlord came in the form of Scotland's 'Braveheart', William Wallace. Although he was born further west, Wallace spent a significant part of his life in Perthshire. He lived in the Carse of Gowrie in his youth and later hid as a guerrilla fighter at Elcho, liberated Scone from English troops and captured Perth castle.

After Wallace's execution in 1305, Robert the Bruce continued the fight for freedom. He seized power by murdering his rival John Comyn and having himself crowned King Robert I of Scotland at Scone on 25 March 1306. His early years as monarch were difficult; he was defeated at the Battle of Methven, just west of Perth, and fled into Highland Perthshire. However, he gradually built up support and retook Perth in 1312 on his way to final victory over the English at Bannockburn in 1314.

The centrality of Perth to Scottish affairs was reinforced when James I convened the first representative parliament here in 1428. But nine years later conspirators murdered the king in his bedchamber in Perth and after that the city lost its prominence. Mary Queen of Scots was another monarch with unhappy connections to Perthshire: she was imprisoned in Lochleven Castle in 1567.

Although there are several battlefield sites around Perthshire, there is little to see at most of them. The 1689 Battle of Killiecrankie, which took place in a narrow pass, is an exception. Here you can view Soldier's Leap, where an escaping redcoat soldier jumped across the River Garry, and a standing stone that marks the spot where the Jacobite leader John

Graham of Claverhouse – better known as 'Bonny Dundee' – died. His tomb is in a ruined chapel in the grounds of Blair Castle.

To quell the troublesome Highlanders, the Black Watch regiment was raised at Aberfeldy. General Wade built the bridge there as part of his Scotland-wide network of military roads, several of which are still visible around Perthshire as tracks through the heather.

The advent of more settled times after the Jacobite rebellions brought gradual changes across Perthshire. For a long time cattle had been the mainstay of the Highland subsistence economy, but demand from the south created a boom in their trade that saw Crieff grow in wealth and importance as the principal market in Scotland. Each autumn, thousands of beasts were herded along grassy drove roads through the glens to converge on the town. Nowadays, the annual event is marked by the Drovers' Tryst walking festival.

As the economy grew, the clan chieftains became wealthy – and usually titled – landowners. Their role transmuted from being tribal leaders to running the old clan lands as vast estates. The Perthshire we see today is a result of their land management practices.

On the one hand, they introduced large-scale sheep farming, which replaced the old cattle-based subsidence farming, leading to depopulation of the glens and preventing regeneration of trees on the already denuded uplands. This left bare hills of grass and heather, scattered with the ruins of shielings, the summer dwellings of the cattle era.

On the other hand, these landowners led the way in systematic tree planting. The Dukes of Atholl, in particular, were famed for creating extensive forests and experimenting with non-native species of tree, such as the European larch. At Blair Castle and Scone Palace there are spectacular arboreta containing trees discovered in the Americas by plant hunters, such as Perthshire men David Douglas and Archibald Menzies.

The contrast created between wild, rugged hills and fertile, wooded valleys appealed to poet and writer alike. Robert Burns toured the area and penned poems about the Falls of Bruar and Birks of Aberfeldy, while Sir Walter Scott described the view of Strathearn from the Ochils as the fairest in all Scotland.

When Queen Victoria visited Perthshire in 1842 she was enchanted by the landscape, which she extolled in her diary. A few years later, the railway arrived and brought with it a burgeoning trade in tourism. Pitlochry and Birnam grew up as resorts and Crieff found a new life as a spa town.

Tourists continue to be important to Perthshire and outdoor recreation is still the major attraction. As in Victorian times, visitors come for the fresh air, pure water and wonderful views. In additional to the traditional field sports of fishing and shooting, a whole new range of outdoor activities have evolved. Cycling and mountain biking, canoeing and white water rafting are now popular sports, though walking continues to be the form of recreation enjoyed by the largest numbers.

The draw of the natural environment has lead to a growth in green tourism, with many visitors coming to see the abundant and accessible wildlife, and to unwind in Perthshire's splendid landscapes. They find an enormous diversity of scenery here, from fertile farmland growing vegetables, fruit and grain, through lush woods and glorious gardens, to high, wild mountains and lonely moors.

Visitors also find a warm welcome from friendly locals who are keen to share their love of Perthshire. The pace of life is slower than in more urban areas, so there is time to exchange the time of day and pass on tips about where to go and what to see. There is also plenty of variety. Each district has its own character and attractions, for instance Blairgowrie is the 'berry capital' of Scotland, while Auchterarder is famous for Gleneagles Hotel and golf courses.

During 20 years of living in Perthshire, I have never tired of travelling around the county and exploring its sights. Although I have written descriptions of more than 250 walks in Perth and Kinross, I am still discovering new routes and fresh views of the lovely countryside. I am sure that, like me, you will find it a source of endless delights.

As you browse the images in this book, you too can journey around the big county. If you are new to Perthshire, you will find that Allan's fine photographs are a marvellous introduction to the area, whilst if you live here, these compelling images will give you fresh perspectives on what is undoubtedly the fairest part of Scotland.

Felicity Martin

27/2/07

Loch Leven Castle. Tucked away on its own island, this impressive stronghold once imprisoned Mary Queen of Scots. Today, it makes a cheerful excursion from Kinross by boat, courtesy of Historic Scotland..

Detail at the foot of the magnificent formal gardens at Kinross House, which were originally laid out and planted between 1679 and 1685 by then owner Sir William Bruce.

At the West End of the Lake [Loch Leven], and the Gardens reaching right down to the very Water's Edge, stands the most beautiful and regular Piece of Architecture (for a private Gentleman's Seat) in all Scotland, perhaps, in all Britain, I mean the House of Kinross. (Daniel Defoe, celebrated author of Robinson Crusoe (1772))

Burleigh Castle, Milnathort. A small 16th-century tower house was a property of the Balfours of Burleigh, who built the castle, from 1446. The Castle was lost in 1757, after the master (and thus his family) fell from grace following a scandal involving forbidden love and a servant girl.

Balvaird Castle, built in 1500 by Sir Andrew Murray of Tullibardine, stands in a commanding location by the A912 near Glenfarg.

Abernethy Round Tower, built in the early 9th century, is one of only two such towers in Scotland. This 22m-tall tower was constructed by monks from the nearby monastery and has been used variously as a place of refuge, a belfry and a sepulchral.

Elcho Castle, now in the care of Historic Scotland, is a less familiar but beautifully preserved and captivating castle tucked away on the south bank of the River Tay near Perth City. Originally built by the Weymss family in 1570, it offers a special sense of how life would have been in those days.

Lower Strathearn displays the rich alluvial pastures and arable lands surrounding the final meanderings of the River Earn, seen here from Moncreiffe by Bridge of Earn.

Looking north from the city bypass. Golf is played at Friarton or Moncreiffe Island with the City of Perth rising behind.

The classic view in rich autumn colour from Kinnoull Hill looking out across the mighty River Tay as it moves into its final and estuarine stage.

Above and opposite: The intensely colourful and stunning garden of Branklyn, seen here in full flush of spring. Originally developed by John and Dorothy Renton with the help of seed collections from plant hunters such as Forrest, Ludlow and Sherriff, it is now superbly maintained by the National Trust for Scotland.

The silvery Tay slips past the classic architecture of the city, seen here from the Perth Bridge.

St John's Place, Perth City.

Barley and berryfields, Glen Carse near Kinfauns.

26   Perthshire

Kilspindie Church, Braes of the Carse.

Springtime, St Leonard's in the Fields and Trinity, Marshall Place.

The River Tay from the tip of Friarton Island looking to Tay Street and the Perth Bridge.

Perth's Museum and Art Gallery, one of the oldest in Britain, houses an impressive collection of art and artifacts.

Scone Palace is immersed in historical significance. Home of the Earls of Mansfield, the site was the capital of the Pictish Kingdom 1500 years ago, as well as being the centre of the ancient Celtic church. Since then it has been the seat of Parliaments and the crowning place of Kings. Until recently it housed the Stone of Destiny, and was immortalised in Shakespeare's Macbeth.

Scone Palace through the north-east entrance, late November at sundown.

Dancing leaves on a fresh and breezy autumn afternoon enhance the elegance of the serene parkland surrounding Scone Palace.

Specimen maple in radiant form, Scone Palace grounds.

The great hedge of Meikleour is an impressive living wall of beech trees over 30 metres high and 520 metres long. Originally planted in 1745, it is officially recorded in the Guinness Book of Records as the highest hedge in the world. Legend has it that Jean Mercer of Meikleour allowed the hedge to grow towards the heavens in memory of her husband Robert Murray Nairne, who was killed at Culloden.

The rear side of the Meikleour Hedge reveals generations of very specific woodland management.

The River Ericht sweeps through Blairgowrie.

Dramatic low light glances across the war memorial in The Wellmeadow, Blairgowrie.

The smart façade of the Royal Hotel Blairgowrie, where generations of merchants, no doubt, have taken refreshment.

Perfect soil and climate have conspired to make Blairgowrie the epicentre of the Scottish raspberry growing district. The distinctive structure of the cane fields can be seen here at Carse of Gowrie.

Alyth, a small county town to the north east of Perthshire, nestles attractively in the rolling lands between Perth and Kirriemuir known as Strathmore.

Glen Taitneach by the Dalmunzie Hotel, Spittal of Glenshee.

Snow fences meander across the high moorland at the off-season ski slopes of Glenshee.

Edradour Distillery by Pitlochry is the smallest distillery in Scotland. An Act in 1823 introduced a minimum legal size for a whiskey still, i.e. just large enough not to be moved and hid. The stills at Edradour are very small - just above the minimum size allowed in the Act.

Late summer, and the fertile lands of Perthshire are strewn with golden straw bales. As a backdrop the spires of the iconic Atholl Palace Hotel, Pitlochry, rise through the morning mist.

The view from the A9 across to the 'Highland Gateway' town of Pitlochry is characterised by the Atholl Palace Hotel and a miniature stand of spindly Scots Pines.

Loch Dunmore by Faskally, Pitlochry. Intense Autumn colour is a real draw to this area at this time of year. This loch is also the venue for the Enchanted Forest Light and Sound Festival. (This picture was taken in the late 1990s; the boathouse has since been refurbished.)

Country House at Faskally, Pitlochry with a rich tapestry of autumn colour as a backdrop.

Looking down on the River Garry from Cammoch Hill, with Killiecrankie and Carn Liath in the distance.

The classic view of the Pass of Killiecrankie in verdant spring colour as seen from the new road bridge over the River Garry.

Swivel 180 degrees from the last view and the River Garry can be seen heading south through big tree country on its way past Pitlochry.

The Southern Banks of Loch Tummel are here characterised by the intense green of the gentle birch.

Loch Tummel and the classic Queen's View must vie for the position of 'most photographed spot in Scotland'. Interestingly, there is no better angle to be had on this view than the one afforded by the official viewpoint, a site carefully managed by the Forestry Commission.

Beautiful trees contribute immensely to the appeal of the 'fair county', and this is nowhere more evident than the point at which Loch Faskally and the River Garry are one and the same body of water, adjacent to Wester Clunie Power station.

Blair Castle, ancient seat of the Earls and Dukes of Atholl, dates back to the 13th century. It sits strategically at the gateway to the Grampian Mountains and the road north to Inverness. The castle is notable for hosting Europe's only remaining private army.

The Atholl Mountains and varied farmland surround the majestic Blair Castle.

The Falls of Bruar offer a delightful stroll along the pine-scented rocky path which follows the Bruar Water as it tumbles through the wooded glen behind the retail phenomenon of the House of Bruar, Blair Atholl.

Dunalastair Water by Kinloch Rannoch is a small loch buffered between the mighty Lochs of Rannoch and Tummel. It is presided over by Schiehallion, the 'fairy hill'.

After rain a gloom lifts from Loch Rannoch, intensifying the scarce colour.

Views from the north shore of Loch Rannoch are greatly enhanced by the perfect peak of Schiehallion, here set off by the delicate stands of native birch.

Mystery pervades this curious little folly perched on a tiny rock island at the western end of Loch Rannoch. This island is actually a crannog called Eilean nam Faoileag. One may muse endlessly as to why it was built - and be impressed that someone actually spared the time and money to create such an object; a little Victorian indulgence, one supposes.

The recently exposed root system relic of a large Scots pine preserved in peat at Loch Eigheach near Rannoch Station.

Loch Laidon, Rannoch Station, and a storm is brewing.

The railway line across Rannoch Moor was built in 1889. It was a most challenging piece of engineering, and at times turf and brushwood were used to till up the bog. The stone carving at Rannoch Station was made by the navvies who built it and is of a Mr Renton, whose timely generosity enabled the line's eventual completion in 1894.

Rannoch Station, full of atmosphere and history, is as remote as a railway station can be.
Here you can see its location in relation to the Glencoe Mountains in the distance.

The Camghouran Burn on the south shore of Loch Rannoch straddles the Black Wood of Rannoch, a substantial remnant of the Great Wood of Caledon.

Loch Rannoch is a classic Highland loch of unsurpassed beauty.

Schiehallion presents an infinite variety of poses - and even here the cattle have great character.

Cattle and oak tree, early one summer morning near Schiehallion Road.

Fortingall is a most surprising village to encounter. What are traditional thatched cottages doing here in Scotland?

Fortingall is a visual delight, a real one-off. It is also home to the most extraordinarily old yew tree - believed to be over 5000 years old.

The crystal waters of the River Lyon snake their way through Glen Lyon.

Glen Lyon supports extensive hill farms with its variety of habitats.

The Roman Bridge in Glen Lyon is an irresistible, almost fairytale, landmark.

The rugged beauty of noble Scots pines in their infinite variety of forms is very much present and well protected here at the Western end of Glen Lyon.

The flood plain of Glen Lyon has created good soil fertility for so wild an environment.

Glen Lyon supports a superb climax beech wood at its eastern end.

More Scots pines prevail, even near the tree line in the remote parts of the Glen.

A lone stag tackles the hill, Glen Lyon, midwinter.

A solitary pine offers shade from a fierce August sun.

Glen Lyon: the longest and most spectacular glen in Scotland.

Near Loch Lyon reservoir, a younger member of an amicable herd of fine Highlanders lazes peacefully among the heather.

The Falls of Dochart, Killin. Depicted in well over a century's worth of picture postcards,
this spectacular site still delivers the goods.

Tup sillouette, south shore of Loch Tay

View to the north shore of Loch Tay from near Ardeonaig.

Highlanders at Loch Tay.

Rowan, Blackface and Croft, north bank of Loch Tay at the foot of Ben Lawers.

Bridge over the Tay, Kenmore.

Kenmore village in full autumn colour.

Golden larches and birches on the banks of Loch Tay, looking to the west from above Kenmore.

The Scottish Crannog Centre at Kenmore, Loch Tay, is a stunningly authentic recreation of a 2,600-year-old Iron Age loch dwelling.

The gentle curve of Loch Tay leads past the dark summit of Ben Lawers to the profile of the mighty Ben More at the head of Glen Dochart.

Winter with Kenmore nestling below an icy Ben Lawers.

Standing stones in the grip of winter at Croftmoraig near Taymouth Castle.

Menzies Castle near Aberfeldy, the beautifully restored seat of the Chiefs of the Menzies Clan, stands proudly by the lush foliage of Weem Wood.

The striking General Wades Bridge over the Tay at Aberfeldy: "... A freestone bridge over the Tay, of five arches, nearly 400 feet in length, the middle arch 60 feet wide, the starlings of oak and the piers and landbreasts founded on piles shod with iron...." (House of Commons Journal, 7th February 1734).

The Birks o' Aberfeldy, the name given to the excellent trail up and down a gorge just outside the town following the visit in August 1787 of Robert Burns, during which he penned his song 'The Birks o' Aberfeldy'.

Strathtay and Grandtully is an exquisite double-barrelled Perthshire village on the banks of the River Tay, famous for whitewater sports but here revealing a more idyllic side to its character.

Strathtay and Grandtully also host gems such as this sweet-scented bluebell wood.

Old Bridge at The Hermitage near Dunkeld, now in the care of the National Trust for Scotland, sits on the banks of the River Braan. It is also home to Ossian's Hall and Ossian's Cave, both Victorian follies, reportedly built by the Dukes of Atholl in the 18th century.

The Falls of Braan, right next to the Ossian's Hall Folly, are spectacular. In season they are also an excellent salmon leap.

Dunkeld. The 'ell' was the original measure for cloth, and now the Ell Shop - pictured here - is run by the National Trust for Scotland.

Dunkeld Cathedral, with its tranquil setting on the banks of the Tay, was at one time the religious centre of Scotland. It was dedicated to St Columba, and his relics were buried under the chancel steps after being brought from Iona.

Birnam Wood and the view to Dunkeld. This forest is celebrated in Shakespeare's Macbeth as the famous Birnam Wood: "Macbeth shall never vanquish'd be until Great Birnam Wood to high Dunsinane hill shall come against him."

Pristine habitat on the shores of the Loch of the Lowes in early morning mist. In 1969, nesting ospreys chose this recently established nature reserve near Dunkeld as their nest site. The birds have been regular annual visitors to the loch ever since, rearing over 50 chicks during that time.

Field of straw bales and an early morning mist rising from the Loch of the Lowes.

The freshwater Loch of Clunie, near Blairgowrie. On the small islet are the ruins of Clunie Castle, a former tower house of the Bishops of Dunkeld.

Sheep graze peacefully alongside the abundant birdlife at Loch Freuchie near Amulree.

Alder trees cling to the banks of the infant River Almond in the wide green strath known as the 'Sma Glen'.

The Buchanty Spout is a spectacular waterfall and salmon leap located deep in the heart of Glen Almond.

Prime steers share this sturdy set of standing stones near Fowlis Wester, Crieff.

Approaching the village of Fowlis Wester.

The replica Pictish carved stone at Fowlis Wester village near Crieff. The original stone can be seen in the adjacent church.

The Lednock Burn tumbles headlong into Glen Lednock.

The extensive Lednock Reservoir near Comrie.

The elaborate but crumbling Monzie Castle gatehouse.

Ben Vorlich in full summer plumage from the north bank of Loch Earn.

Tranquil Loch Voil is, strictly speaking, in Stirlingshire - but there is strong conviction to support the view that in spirit it is very much still part of Perthshire.

Loch Voil from the Braes of Balquidder, emanating a curious cloud inversion.

Farm at Edinample, Loch Earn.

Soft summer light illuminates a small tributary of the River Earn as it flows past the fort at Dundurn near St Filans.

Looking across to Comrie village from the monument by The Milton.

Built in 1805, 'The White Church' of Comrie is a Grade A listed building, which lies at the heart of this historic conservation village.

Traditional hardware shop in the High Street, Crieff.

James Square and the elaborate fountain from the Drummond Hotel, Crieff.

The magnificent ornamental gardens surrounding Drummond Castle.

The stunningly symmetrical formal garden of Drummond Castle near Crieff.

The world-renowned Gleneagles Golf Course and Country Club.

Gleneagles Hotel is a world-class, world-famous luxury hotel.

The village of Dunning.

Storm clouds and late sun pick out the vernacular village style architecture of Bridgend, Dunning.